Right Where You Are

Encouragement Journal

Tammy Helfrich

ISBN-13: 978-0692738054

ISBN-10: 0692738053

DEDICATION

This journal is dedicated to YOU. I want to encourage you to be FULLY you, and to live into who you were created to be.

I have been on a journey of learning to truly know myself and understand how I am wired. It has taken me a long time to fully believe and appreciate that I am a natural encourager. I absolutely love seeing the good in others and pointing it out to them. I want people to believe and see who they really are.

I see hidden potential in everyone. I see where you are holding back, and I see where you still have room to grow in believing you are great at something. And even though I can't physically see you right now, I know you have something beautiful to offer the world. It just takes time to uncover it and truly believe it.

I encourage you to make this journal your own. Write, sketch, color and dream on the pages in a way that suits you best. I've included encouraging words and quotes as my gift to you.

I believe in you. You have something amazing to bring when you show up as the real you. But it starts with believing in yourself. My wish is that the words will help you in the exact moment you need to read them.

I truly believe life begins right where you are.

ACKNOWLEDGMENTS

This journal is the result of years of learning how to be more intentional with my gift of encouragement.

I didn't always believe my words mattered or were very encouraging. But now I know that's simply not true. A few encouraging words can make all the difference to someone at just the right time.

I have been encouraged by so many people who read my blog, listen to my podcast, Right Where You Are, and interact with me in the online world. Thank you for being you and being a part of my life.

I am so honored to have such an incredible community around me. I am surrounded by creative leaders, friends and people who continue to challenge me to become who I've been created to be. I can't imagine being on this journey without all of you. Thank you.

I am so thankful for my husband Rick, who inspires me and challenges me to live a life of adventure and creativity. I love the life we've created and look forward to sharing many more years of fun together.

There are two special boys who have brought so much joy, love, and fun into my life. Jonah and Kaden - I am so thankful I get to be your mom. Your big hearts and creative nature continue to challenge me to be fully me, and I love experiencing life with you!

You matter. Even when you don't feel it or believe it.

You matter simply because you are here.

Right now.

Right where you are.

You are **AWESOME**.

Believe it.

Right where you are is **EXACTLY** where you are supposed to be.

You can make a difference to someone today, simply by being **YOU**.

YOU are the magic ingredient you are searching for.

Nobody else has **YOUR** answers.

Choose to show up today.

Live each moment and embrace life in a new way.

Be awesome **NOW**.

Be curious and loving to yourself.

This is the only way to uncover your answers hidden within.

Do more of what makes you come **alive.**

Trust your inner wisdom.

Believing in yourself is a process.

Don't rush it.

Practice it every day until it becomes automatic.

There is only one you.

Celebrate who you are!

Your **creativity** is a gift.

Cherish it!

You are the only one who can **decide** to live your life.

You **can't** hate yourself _____.

(Trust me!)

Loving yourself is the **greatest gift** you can ever give.

You have been equipped with everything you need to do what **makes you come alive**.

You just need to take the next step.

Keep bringing **all of YOU** to the world.

It makes everything more awesome.

Keep being **AWESOME!**

What lights you up?

Oceans?

Nature?

Creating?

Take the time to **do more** of it today.

Control is an illusion.

The **real magic** happens
when we learn to
surrender to something
bigger than ourselves.

You **can** do this.

Life is meant to be lived,
not just endured.

Do something that makes
you feel alive today.

Rest.

Slow down.

Take a **breath**.

You've got this.

Be as **patient** with yourself as you are with those you love.

Love **yourself** well today.

We can't become who we were created to be if we don't **believe** in ourselves.

Life doesn't just happen to us.

We get to **create it**.

How can you take one step towards creating the life you desire today?

Are you doing something to **get your own attention**?

Spend some time thinking about what that looks like in your life.

Do the **next** right thing.

You are **more powerful** than you give yourself credit for.

Take back your power.

Awareness with loving compassion and curiosity is a totally different space than judgment and condemnation.

Choose to be curious about yourself today.

The **present** is all we have.

Be present today.

You **don't** have to stay stuck in the "I don't know" trap.

Take the next step that you do know.

We **always** have a choice of how we think about something.

Choose wisely.

YOU have what it takes.

I promise.

ABOUT TAMMY

I have learned that my words can encourage and help someone at just the right time. I've learned that by sharing my story and experience, I can help people who need to know they are not alone.

This has been a journey for me. I left a successful career in sales in order to follow my heart and invest in people. That decision has impacted me in ways that I could not have possibly imagined. I've had to dive deep into my own life and do the work of getting healthy emotionally and spiritually in order to allow my work to flow as a natural expression of me.

I write, coach, speak and host a podcast called Right Where You Are. I help people understand they can create the life they truly desire simply by learning to clear their mind clutter and uncover the deep-seeded beliefs that are holding them back.

I love to meet people who are living into who they are created to be, and who are wanting to make transformational change in their life. I believe that we can all change the world by being our authentic selves and making a difference in the world around us. Right where we are.

Thank you for taking the time to journal and invest in YOU. You are worth it!

www.tammyhelfrich.com

35028196R00051

Made in the USA
Middletown, DE
01 February 2019